T0380702

YOUNG AT HEART
YOUNG IN SPIRIT

Artwork by Samuel T Young 1877 ~1952
Verse by Wesley R Withers

This book is a work of non-fiction. Unless otherwise noted, the author and the publisher make no explicit guarantees as to the accuracy of the information contained in this book and in some cases, names of people and places have been altered to protect their privacy.

WestBow Press books may be ordered through booksellers or by contacting:

WestBow Press
A Division of Thomas Nelson & Zondervan
1663 Liberty Drive
Bloomington, IN 47403
www.westbowpress.com
1 (866) 928-1240

ISBN: 978-1-9736-6562-5 (sc)
ISBN: 978-1-9736-6563-2 (e)

Library of Congress Control Number: 2019907544

Print information available on the last page.

WestBow Press rev. date: 08/15/2019

Folk Art, Poetry, Reflection of times gone by, Faith, Inspiration, Suffering, Love, Courage, Tributes or History. I'm not sure what you will make of this collection. All I can tell you is how this book came to be. What you do with it is up to you. My prayer is that this will bring you peace, perspective and inspiration.

Samuel T. Young was my Great Grandfather. He was never famous, outside of Manheim Pennsylvania. He certainly was never rich by most earthly measures, and he was struck down in his prime as a brick layer with what we as a family have always called "Crippling Arthritis" or what is more accurately known as "Rheumatoid Arthritis". Today, with modern medicine, he would have enjoyed a much more normal life. But in 1898, medical science had not yet conquered the disease that would destroy his body over the next 54 years. In fact, he would go on to spend nearly forty years completely bed-ridden with his knees locked in place at a forty-five degree angle, and his hands looking as though they were frozen around objects none of us could ever see or hold.

My first introduction to his memory was his coffee table. It is possibly the ugliest piece of furniture you would ever see. Made of wood and shorter than a love seat. It has always sat in front of my Mother's spot where she reads and does her cross stitch. My second memory has been the many drawings that my mother "Sarah", affectionately called "Sally" by Grampa Young, has had framed and hung about on the walls of my childhood home. "Mummer" as I call her, also had a loose collection of his drawings of which I was permitted to peruse from time to time. Grampa Young was a committed diarist. Keeping track of current events, letters he had written and guests who had visited him. He wrote many a commentary for the local newspapers and was known for his sharp wit. And of course, there were the stories from my family. My Grandmother, and my Aunts and Uncles who have kept his memory alive.

I couldn't draw a straight line with a ruler, and if you could measure my artistic talent with a scale, you might need to have a negative side, but I must have inherited his talent to write poetry, though in all of his writings I only ever found the one included in this book. I have carried that in the safest place through all of my life, in the darkest of times, when I felt I had nothing left; I pulled it from my heart. If a man who lived with pain so bad that he needed morphine when he was overwhelmed, could draw the drawings you will see, and write the poem contained in this book, then you too can find the courage to face your reality.

From the front room at his home on main street in Manheim, he would use his colored pencils to draw the many drawings we as a family have treasured for nearly a century. But he also made sure that the soldiers from Manheim serving in both World Wars, including at one point, four of his eight sons; received homemade postcards and letters. He sought to inspire then, as he continues to do so today. Samuel had laid up his treasures in heaven, where neither moss nor rust doth corrupt, but his illness prevented him from creating any real wealth here on earth.

Many people would visit him on a daily and weekly basis, one such person was ol' Doc Brenner. She was a true friend to our family and provided care for him during much of his illness without ever charging a dime for her services. Dr. Brenner was also my family doctor for the early part of my life. I remember going in for my kindergarten vaccinations and she was worried how I would handle the needles. To help build my courage, she asked me what shape scar I would like; a boat, plane or race car, because that would help her choose which needle. I still can't help but smile at what my grandmother would call a "Tarydiddle" or fib. Anyway, Doc Brenner came to the house to give Grampa his morphine injections and keep him free of bedsores, house-calls at no charge!

Because my Grandfather Arthur Nelson and Grandmother Mabel took care of him, they all lived together in a duplex house with my mother and Uncle Frank "Frit" in the latter years. My grandfather was the local barber and made sure Grampa Samuel was turned out properly with his hair cut and a fresh straight razor shave once a week. Arthur and Mabel raised seven children in that house with births that spanned over a twenty-year period. When Grampa Young was at his sickest, he was at home with the two youngest grandchildren, my mother, and uncle.

One of their favorite memories, besides sitting on either side of him and listening to his stories was playing hide and seek.... But how do you play hide and seek with a bedridden man???

Hide N Seek With Grampa Young

While Samuel stayed put in his front room lair.
Listening for Sally and Frit with great care;
With a gleam in his eye he heard every giggle!
But pretended not to hear every chair squeak and wiggle.
They crawled through the house,
Searching for just the right spot;
A place to rest that was never too cool or too hot
Then doing their best imitation of a little town mouse
Are you next to the wooden kitchen chair?
If yes you must return to my front room lair!
No papa we aren't they said with a grin.
And now you must pull a hair from your chinney chin chin!
Are you next to the deep kitchen stainless steel sink?
He tilted his head as he pondered to think.
No papa we aren't they both nodded and winked.
Strike two Papa now you owe us a kiss on the cheek!
I know I know, I figured it out!
You will come here soon, with a smile not a pout.
You are next to the cabinet with wood made from teak.
With that miniature bird with a colorful beak.
Oh Papa Oh Papa,
You figured us out!
Kiss us both on the cheek,
We promise, no pouts.

There were a great many townspeople that came to visit Grampa Young, all with designs in their head that they were on a mission to cheer him up. But a man that has joy, needs no cheering up. And when they left, they realized it was them that was taking home more courage, strength and joy than they had brought with them. Yet how could I know this, he passed away fourteen years before my own birth? Simple. His drawings! I have seen every single surviving drawing known to exist, and there is no evidence of despair or anger in any one of them. Nothing but the reflection of God's love and compassion which compelled him to live with joy. I know because of his poem which was the window into his suffering, which he accepted as God's gift, even though he could not understand the reason for his suffering, he did realize the benefit of suffering. His diaries contained no evidence of anger towards God for his ailment. And finally, his legacy, which continues on through his family through his lessons of Christian faith, service to others, kindness, generosity, integrity, work ethic and determination.

About ten years ago, Christmas was rapidly approaching when I got the idea that I would take one of my four original "Christmas" postcards and scan and copy them on cardstock to emulate the originals. I wrote a poem to accompany the drawing and sent them to my family members. To say I was overwhelmed by the response would be an understatement, but what was even funnier was how many people thought I had given them an "original" postcard drawing. By August of the next year, I was already receiving requests for another card, which I did. By June of the next year, I was receiving more requests and I knew I had several problems; I had created a demand to keep producing these Christmas cards of which I only had a few drawings, and that there was a real need to keep these drawings relevant to my extended family.

Except for a few hand selected drawings that had been given to me and my three siblings, the bulk of his drawings were in the possession of my Mother and My Aunt Julia, who kept her drawings locked up tighter than Fort Knox. There was always good reason to do so, because these are pencil drawings, the acid in the paper is slowly eating the carbon from the pencils, thus we are losing them because we don't want to handle them, and the younger generation doesn't get to understand their legacy because they don't have access to the drawings. So, I made the decision to write this book, for "Mummer", my son, the next generation and now you.

It took months to scan, color correct and try to brighten, sharpen and ready the images for reproduction. Then one day, I simply sat down and started placing images to a page and writing the poems that accompany them. The greatest compliment I receive is when people mistake my words for my Grampa's. That means that I have captured his voice, his spirit, and most importantly, his joy.

Final thoughts; my Grampa was not a professional artist. These drawings were done by a man who had pencils stuck in the valleys between his fingers. He never went to France to study art with "Monet". He laid bricks. Finally, I hope you will purchase this book to take up residence on your coffee table, just like it has on my Mummer's. But by the way, her coffee table isn't a coffee table, it was Grampa's wooden stretcher. Which was built by my grandfather to take Samuel to visit his sons and daughters every summer.

In times of good and times of bad
I'm thankful for the life and family I've had
My feet are still, my hands are stiff
My mind is still sharp, evidence God's gift.
There's no tv, only radio
But my memories entertain me and keep me on the go
Though far from the battlefields
I'm racked with pain
But prayer for the wounded I count as gain
My boys are at war and my daughters are here
I write them each letters to stem back the tears
Frit's at my side with Sally at my feet
Mabel's in the kitchen cooking something to eat
What a great inheritance
This family of mine
Just take it all in
Before you run out of time

Been off fishin the Chiques.
Just check out my Trout!
Got two to the bank…
Could I have had more? Check out my pout!

By the seat of my pants,
That bear's got me again.
With no fruit in the tree,
Guess I go hungry again!
Next time we shortcut
I'll head up the tree first!
And you'll see how much for your denim…
that bear thirsts!

Life through a window requires much concentration, a joyful spirit and much imagination. When life seems bleak, in black and white. I reach for my pencils and paper near right. This vivid recollection comes courtesy of color, from the green of the trees to the yellow hay stubble. The ghosts of my childhood come roaring back, characters and friends, fishin and ridin horseback. Progress has come to my hometown Manheim, though I could have been anywhere, it is good to be where I'm. Dusty straight streets, houses of brick and my church on the corner. Straight beautiful fences of stone held with mortar.

A curious thing happened on my walk up Main Street.

A woman was feedin the chickens while the man hid his feet.

The goat and the mule looked on the action with glee,

But his nephews kept their eyes centered on me.

Mom keeps on working, no time for to stop, Will that dog catch his pockets?

Well there goes that dog again… rip, tear and pop.

Pop lands a blow on the nose of that dog and says "momma I guess you just got another ol' job."

Mind my supper first, clear the table and then. Wipe up the dishes and the frying pan.

Before turning in, with time well spent, pick up that needle and with thread fix that rent!

★★★★★★★★★★

The Tin Roof Hymn Sing Association

No experience necessary!

Must be willing to work late.

Volume a must.

BYOC "bring your own catnip"

★★★★★★★★★★

He with crooked fingers drew,
The Joy through pain, his life he knew.
Confined to bed, his place a cell.
His dreams grew bigger with stories yet to tell!
An audience of "Young'uns" sat at his feet.
His desire to encourage made his heart beat!
No Nobler mission on earth was found.
To find God's joy, through love abound.
Don't miss the message of this life led.
No peace is permanent without He who bled.
~WRW 2007

A WINTER'S PROMISE

~November 2008~

Looking through my window; the Sun's in full bloom.
It's neither spring nor summer, but a cold winter's noon.
The silvery presence of frost on the cold window pane.
Reminds me that my hands are frozen in place from the pain.
But before Triumph comes; you must first pay the cost.
Like a mother with child; who without labor is lost.
Yet Hope springs eternal as Salvation is too!
And Love triumphs evil, the lonely feelings of blue.
Wise men still seek him, even to this day!
He's never far away unless you keep Him at bay.
Christ has come, His birth on this date.
But, unless He's your Savior, danger is yours through the wait.
Invite Him in now and this discovery is yours.
As a soldier, home from battle is no longer on tour.
Home to the love and joy now found.
A journey to Heaven where grace & peace will abound.
Choose you this day whom you will serve.
Cry out to Heaven if you haven't the nerve!
For when my hands start to hurt and my joints with pain bleed.
I look to the cross and I have all I need!
~WRW 2008
Inspired by Samuel T. Young

01/02/1877 – 09/20/1952

Departed

YOUNG, Samuel T., entered the land of perfect rest at the age of 75 years, 7 months and 18 days following an illness of crippling arthritis of 54 years, more than 30 of which he was bedfast. Brother Sam had a glowing Christian personality which gave him a marvelous victory over his physical condition. No person has ever talked with Sam Young who did not experience the release of his burden as his soul burst forth with praise to Almighty God because of the testimony of Brother Sam. Shut-ins all over the country were cheered and encouraged because when Brother Sam knew of someone who needed a friend, he wrote a letter with his crippled fingers, which brought the grace of God into the heart of the reader. Truly Brother Sam had a fruitful, spirit-filled ministry in spite of the wasting away of his body, the constant pain, and never leaving his bed for more than thirty years. His mind was active and filled with the love of God; his soul grew to proportions few of us can hope to attain. His wife, the former Mary Knier died several years ago. He is survived by the following children: Phares, Paul, Frank, Russel, Elmer, Robert and Mrs. Arthur Nelson with whom he lived; and the following sister and brothers: Mrs. Wayne Stauffer, Atty, A. H. Young, Rev. C. E. Young, and Dr. D. E. Young, District

I know not why
His hand is laid,
In chastening on my life.
Nor why it is my little world,
Is filled so full of strife.
I know not why,
When faith looks up,
And seeks for rest from pain.
That o'er my skies,
Fresh clouds arise,
And drench my path with rain.
I know not why
my prayer so long,
By Him has been denied.
Nor why, while others' ships sail on, mine
should in port abide.
But I do know that God is Love,
and He my burden shares
And though I may not understand,
I know for me He Cares!
~Samuel T Young

"An empty pot"

Mother I went huntin.

Walked way out in the woods.

Kept my eyes peeled all day…

But I swear I didn't see nothin!

"A New School For Manheim"

Out on East High Street,
I work with trowel in hand.
A safe and wonderful place to learn,
Where ignorance makes no stand!
Teachers who love children.
And with firm and gentle touch,
Guide my great grandchildren
To great achievement
through hard work, but never luck.
In just a few more years, a trowel won't fit my hands,
My strength will leave me weak
but my legacy will always stand

MANHEIM FARMSHOW

SEPTEMBER IS IN THE BOOKS, THE CORN HAS ALL BEEN PICKED.
IN THE FIELD BESIDE THE HIGH SCHOOL OUT BY CHIQUES CREEK.
FIND FUNNEL CAKES AND HORSE PULLEN!
AND GIRLS IN SUNDAY'S BEST.
ALL COME OUT TO BE SEEN WHILE STROLLEN.
AND CATCH THE MAN WHO'S BEST!
THERE'S MUSIC, GAMES AND LAUGHTER.
NO BETTER TIME IS HAD.
THE WRESTLIN TEAM IS HUNGRY!
AND ELIZABETHTOWN IS SAD.

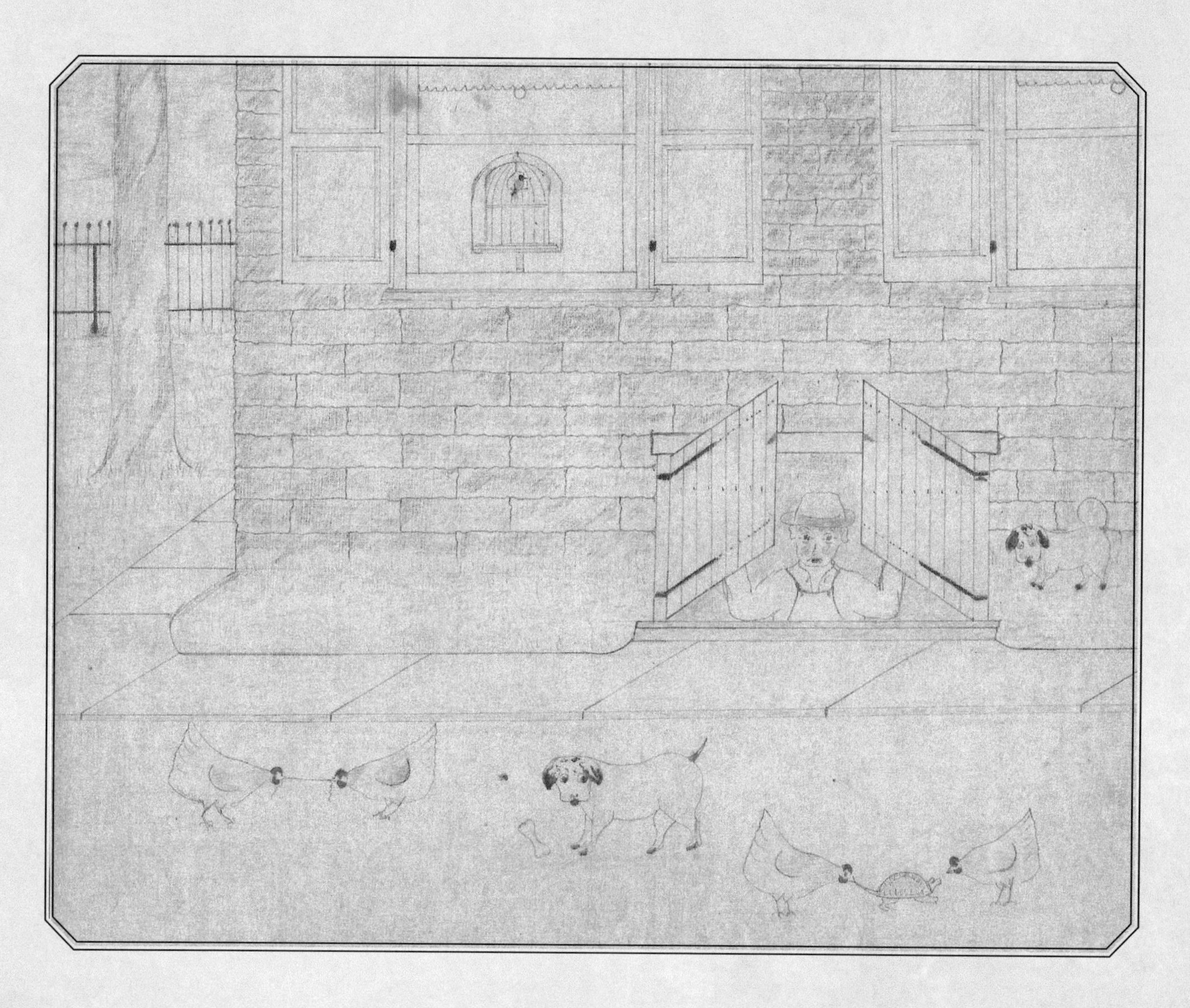

Daddy's in the basement, he says he's working hard.
But I just caught him peeking at a turtle in the yard!
He thinks the turtles got trouble, and he's running with all his might.
But if he don't do what momma said, he's in for a long cold night!

"It aint so funny when he has you by the pants huh!
Hey, do you suppose he is just after that jerky in your pocket

Be Careful what you fish for when you cast in full sun light
With four friends skinny dippin, a full moon's out tonight!
Ole Billy's the one conservative sittin' on the bank,
With his faithful friend that "Winston" the british bulldog on his right.
While Pete and Johnny whip their poles they yell with all their might!
Stop all that divin' and splashin…
Your givin' the fish a fright!

Out by the bulrush, the ducks swim round and round,
In front of the boat I sit with Abe and his faithful curl tailed hound.
Those ducks they are so pretty, What a wonderful mount they'd make.
I'd catch one and take him home if only they'd stop swimming 'round this lake.

I guess I don't have to outrun that hungry bear! I just have to outrun you!

I hate the rain!
It makes me feel so blue.
Thank goodness for umbrellas,
For I'll sit here dry and stew.
Cheer up says the crazy heron,
You can only get so wet!
The fishin' is best when it's raining,
On that you can place your bet!

I think I'll head out to Hernley's church to visit the family plot.
Mary's there and she waits patiently, but I miss her so much
That her memory still haunts me.
All our days spent together as her man and she my wife,
We worked so well together as fork does so with knife.
Up, up the hill, the driveway on left, edging close to her headstone
And I can't catch my breath, I look to the sky, whisper a prayer right then,
Her voice calls to me saying "please return as soon as you can".

Ridin' the team with my wide brim hat.
Ready to work, no doubt about that!
Up with the roosters, a long day ahead.
Sam's in the wagon; alongside runs old Fred.
We'll be pick'n potatoes till we can't stand up straight.
We won't lie back down till a quarter to eight!

Christmas Greetings
Merry
Christmas.

Merry
Christmas

Merry
Christmas
To
You.

Christmas
Greetings.

You wanted a sample of something I've written.
A Long time ago I slid on a diamond and was smitten.
There's no sound more pure, than the crack of a bat!
Unless it's your pitcher putting the other guy on the mat.

In the early days of my youth nothing could keep me away-
"Cmon, it'll clear up", of course it's raining sideways...
Batting practice, grounders, situational baseball,
Home games, away games, the thrill of it all!

We all dreamed of being "Hammerin Hank".
With a mighty blow that ball we would spank!
Baseball was the first sport to embrace integration.
Where men of all color earned the respect of our Nation.
Boys didn't judge by the color of their skin,
They just saw their heroes who worked hard to win.
Using God given skills, and a lot of hard work,
They bring us together on a field made of dirt.

That ram drives me crazy, always sneakin up on me..
But with two skates and a pillow,
My problem's left behind me!
I' ll head down to the corner.
To visit with Mom & Pop at Rettews!
And buy some penny candy and one or two Charleston chews.
Then head back to the diamond.
To peek through the knothole in the fence!
I'll catch the last two innings of the game with my Best friend Spence!
The "Unhusked Nine" are favored against those little po's!
But don't count 'em out just yet they've got courage from head to toe!

In like a lion, out like a lamb.
I dream of the ocean with tan colored sand…
Cooped up all winter, I'm ready for change!
Shuck the long underwear for now it feels strange.
Away with the hats; stow all those gloves.
Break out the swim trunks and fly like a dove!

Grampa was a democrat
I'm sure I don't know why.
The mere thought of such a travesty
Brings a tear to my eye.
I guess like any card player
He wanted a new deal.
But with 75 years of hindsight
I just want repeal!

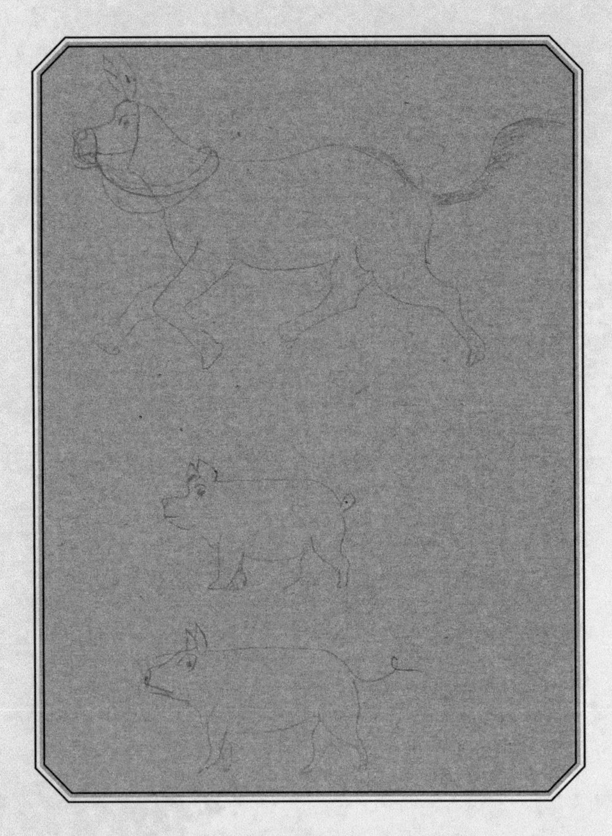

Out on the farm, six pigs with curly tails,
Two chickens fight over corn meal whilst I fork hay bales.
Daddy must be hidin', an the barn's a perfect spot.
But if we don't feed these porkchops now!
Come winter, there's nothin in the pot!

Sowing in the morning, sowing seeds of kindness, Sowing in the noontide and the dewy eve;

Waiting for the harvest, and the time of reaping, We shall come rejoicing, bringing in the sheaves. Bringing in the sheaves, bringing in the sheaves, We shall come rejoicing, bringing in the sheaves;

Bringing in the sheaves, bringing in the sheaves, We shall come rejoicing, bringing in the sheaves.

~David Rose Bringing in the sheaves

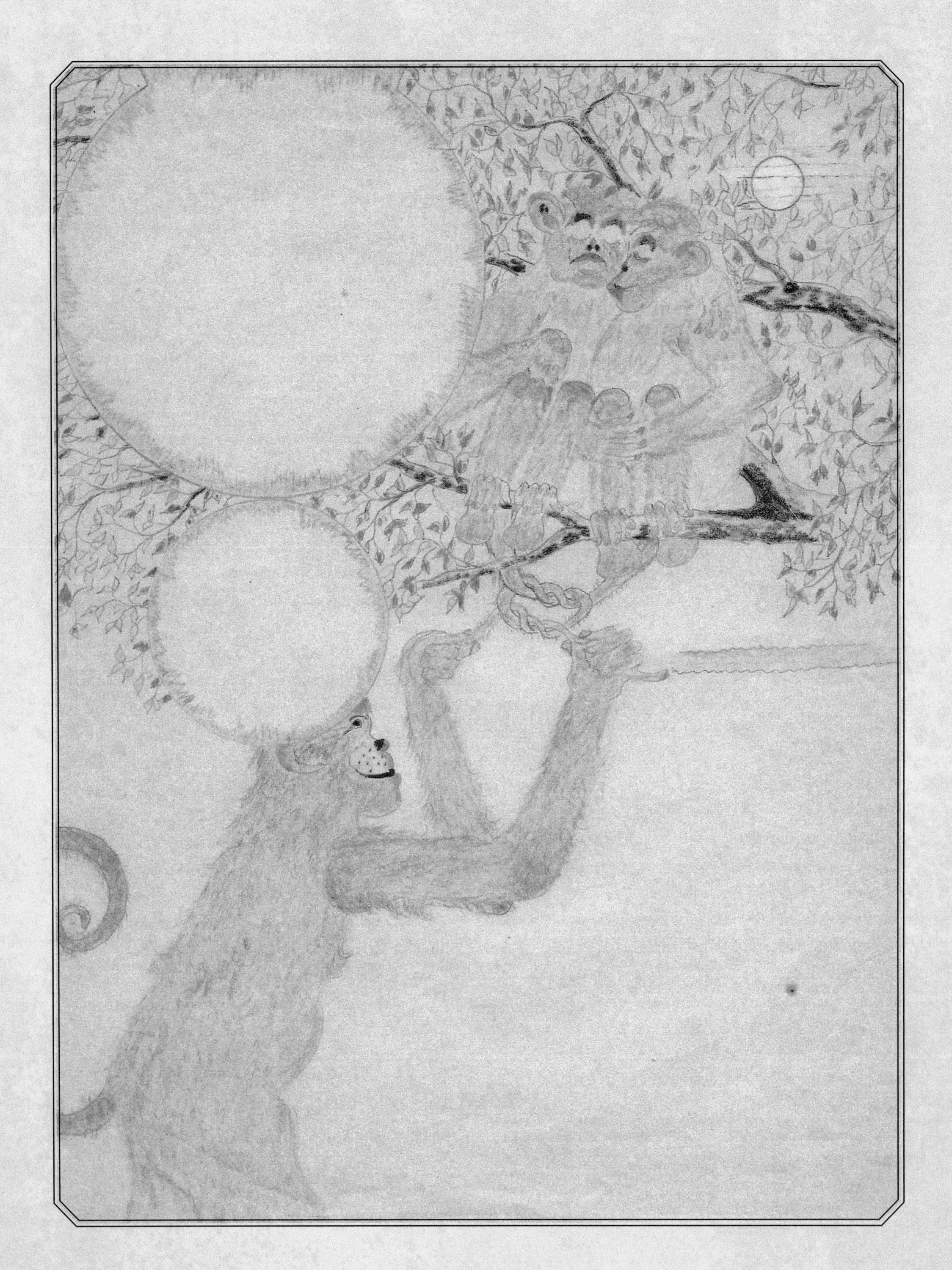

Monkeyshines

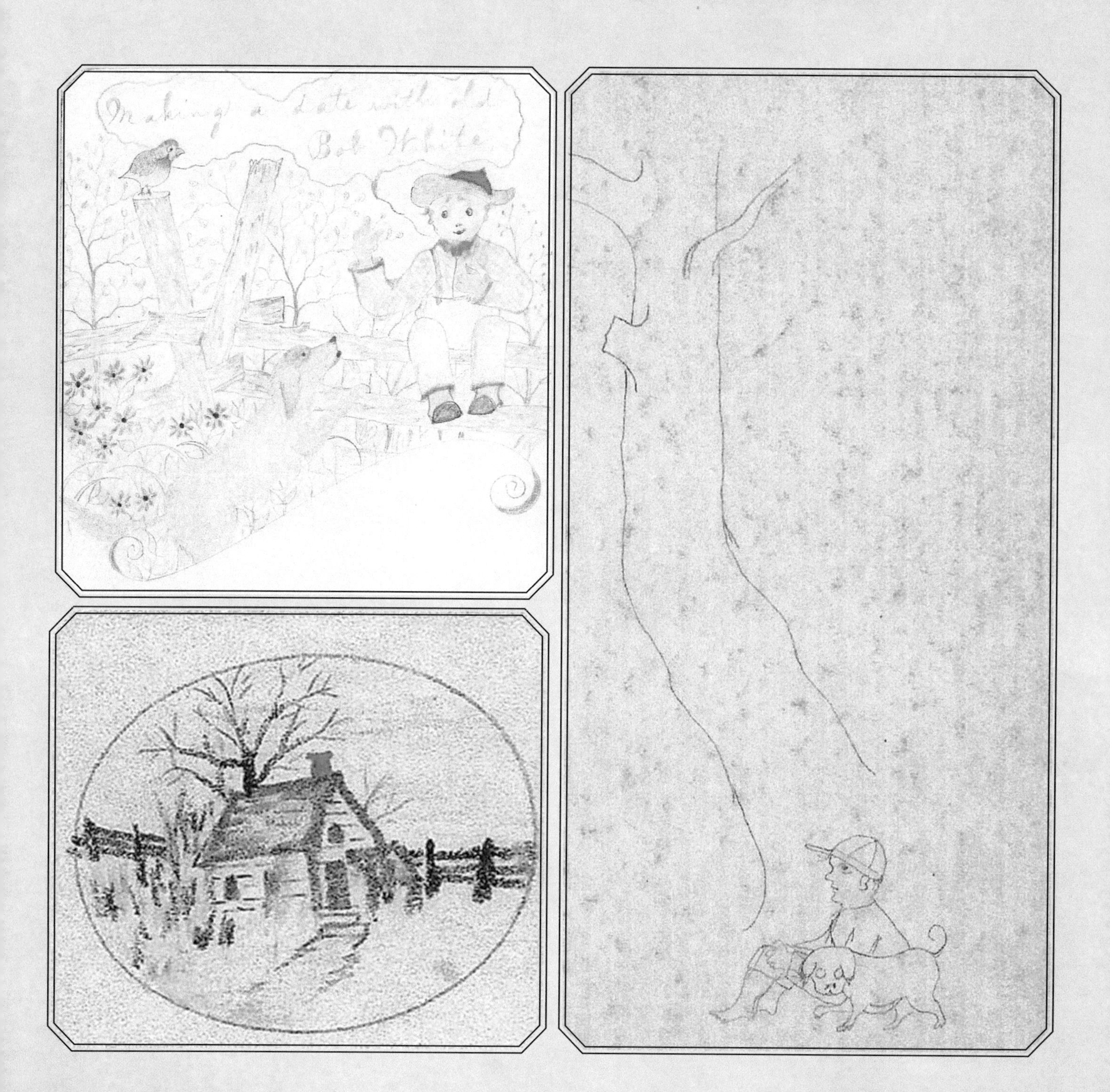
Making a date with old
Bob White

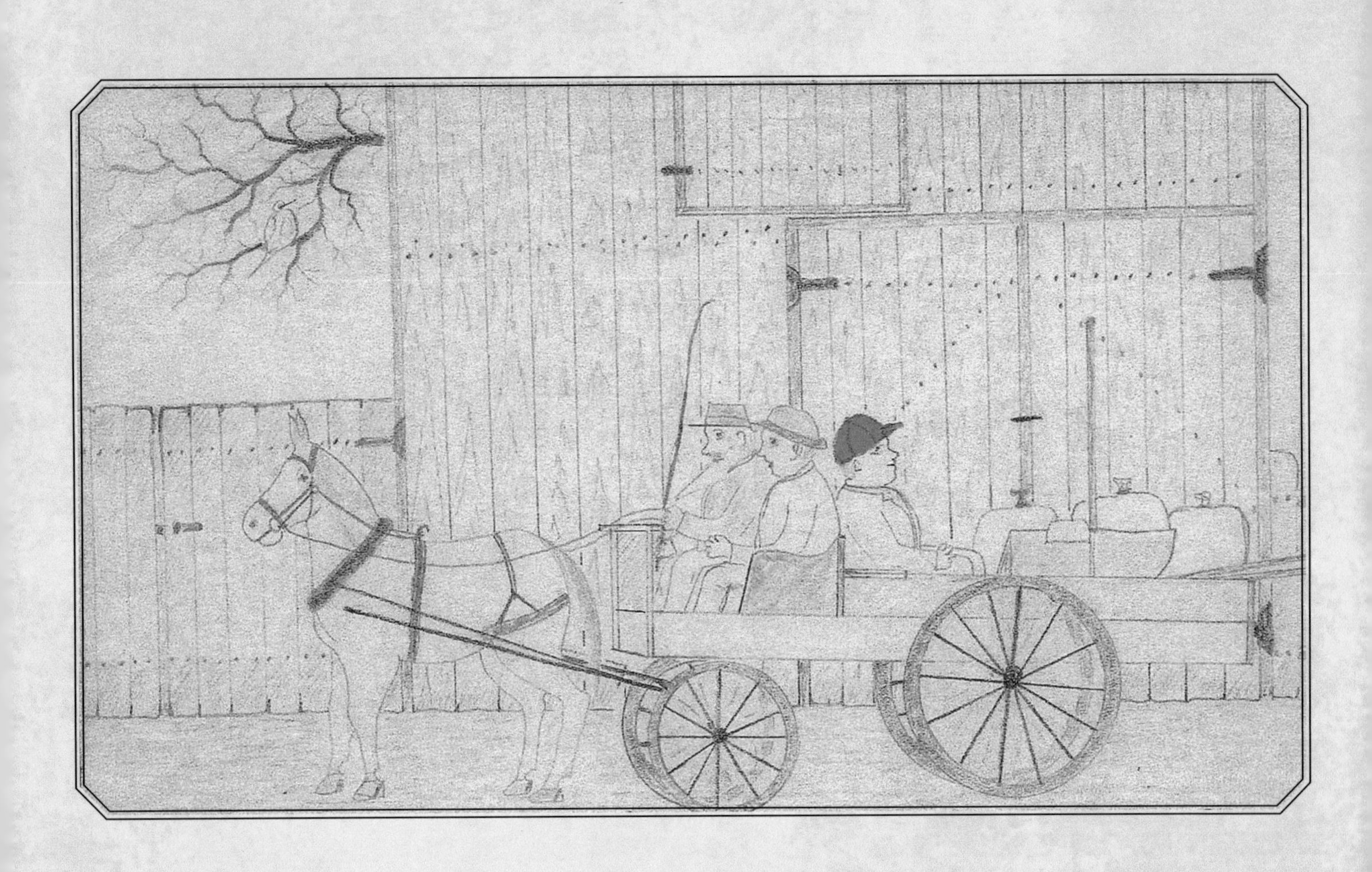

SALT
XXX
SNAKE BITE.
SONG RESTORER.

Country Mail

S T Young

House Cleaning Time
Mary in sunbonnet with her swishing, swooshing broom
Has routed all the spiders from their cosy dens of gloom.
The dust and dirt are taking flight, the carpet runs away
The dog has chased you up a tree, and Old Bill joins the fray.
Paul hops the fence and off he goes, but Elmer's locked Inside
Scared stiff of course. Now Bossy moos while Old Sol's grin is wi
He knows the Hous Botz Gichters will pack up and fly away
And that the Spiders and the dirt will soon come back to stay.

Saturday Jan 5th '35
S. J. J.

Dream House

Any place with family, is a place to lay my head.
Walls to hang some pictures above a queen- sized bed.
Laughter reigns supreme, we're playing cards tonight!
It's always about the family, for that alone is right.

COLLABORATION

When Sam and Jully make a book you never know for what to look.
Jull says its often hard ta find what Sam, the artist, had in mind.
Sam says that Jull can never see his point however plain it be,
For she will take a little scene and make it what it doesn't mean!
Says Jully, like Sam's rabbit fleet, in "OUR BOOK" sense and nonsense meet;
They get acquainted for a while then part, but if they leave a smile
And back to Sam some Mem'ries bring, then "OUR BOOK" is a pleasant thing.
Heigho, Inspector! we're "in print" leaf thru these pages, take a squint
At all the pickters you have made... Impressive? Hmm! It's some parade!
Some go'way back to '29 and most of them are mighty fine.
This is my tribute to the Hours you gave to me thru sun and showers.
The most unusual things you know, we're hearing every day — and so —
Here is the one that's SELDOM heard:

I'm giving you
The FINAL WORD!

Yours with love
for happy hours of reading,
Jully

rch 8, 1946.

goodnight
J.
Sam.

Author Biography

Wesley has a Masters Degree in Divinity from Emmanuel Theological Seminary, but has worked most of his life in sales and marketing. Married to his wife Carrie, they have one son, Jared and live on an island in Maine.

"Wesley does a masterful job of transporting us into the world of his Great Grandfather Samuel. It is inspiring to re-discover the simple joys of family, farming, fishing, hunting and community that had to be recreated from memory because of the disease that destroyed his body but not his faith! A must have in these challenging times!"

Remain strong and keep the faith!

Phil 3:10

Dr. Samuel A. Thomas
President & CEO
Hopegivers International

"I believe that this book deserves to be in every Doctor's office, Nursing home, and on every coffee table across America! Why, because Samuel and Wesley do a masterful job of reminding us to take in the Glory that the Lord has made! I've personally heard Wesley tell the story of his Great Grandfather's suffering and how he ministered to the soldiers with his drawings, and it is refreshing. Wesley might not be able to draw, but he has captured the voice of the greatest generation that lived through two world wars and the great depression, teaching us how to return to faith, family, love and yes, laughter!"

Dr. Joel Lampe
International Director and Senior Curator of the Bible Museum, is continuing the work started by his father, Dr. Craig Lampe. Joel Lampe also hosts the Christian program "He Chose You" and co-hosted Telly Award-winning specials "How We Got the Bible" and "The Bible on Trial.